Washington

JE

Ocelots

By Sam Dollar

Steadwell Books

Raintree Steck-Vaughn Publishers

A Harcourt Company

Austin · New York
www.steck-vaughn.com

ANIMALS OF THE RAIN FOREST

Published by Raintree Steck-Vaughn Publishers, an imprint of Steck-Vaughn Company.

Library of Congress Cataloging-in-Publication Data
Cataloging-in-Publication data is available upon request.

Produced by Compass Books

Photo Acknowledgments
Corbis/Tom Brakefield, 22; Wolfgang Kaehler, 24; George Lepp, 28
    Tony Rath Photography, 4-5, 11, 12, 13, 15, 16, 26
Unicorn Stock Photos/Marie Mills & David Cummings, cover
Visuals Unlimited/Joe McDonald, title page; John Gerlach, 8, 19; Glen M.
    Oliver, 20

Content Consultants
Dr. Cynthia Sims Parr
Research Associate
University of Michigan Museum of Zoology

Maria Kent Rowell
Science Consultant
Sebastopol, California

David Larwa
National Science Education Consultant
Educational Training Services
Brighton, Michigan

Contents

Range Map for Ocelots 6

A Quick Look at Ocelots 7

Ocelots in the Rain Forest 9

Hunting and Eating 17

An Ocelot's Life Cycle 21

Living with Ocelots 25

Glossary 30

Internet Sites and Useful Addresses 31

Index 32

UNITED STATES
OF AMERICA

MEXICO

BELIZE
HONDURAS
GUATEMALA   NICARAGUA
EL SALVADOR   Caribbean
                    Sea

COSTA RICA

PANAMA   VENEZUELA

COLOMBIA

ECUADOR

North
Atlantic
Ocean

GUYANA
SURINAME

FRENCH
GUIANA
(FRANCE)

PERU

AMAZON
RIVER

BRAZIL

BOLIVIA

South
Pacific
Ocean   PARAGUAY

CHILE   South
                                         Atlantic
                                         Ocean

ARGENTINA   URUGUAY

Range of the
Ocelot

Surrounding
Land

Water

N
W ✦ E
S

Borders

Rivers

A Quick Look at Ocelots

What do ocelots look like?
Ocelots are small, wild cats. They have spotted yellow fur and ringed markings on their tails.

Where do ocelots live?
Most ocelots live in and around the rain forests of South America. Some also live in Central America and southern parts of North America.

What do ocelots eat?
Ocelots eat other animals. They hunt mostly small rodents. A rodent is a mammal with four special, sharp front teeth used for biting on things. Ocelots also eat birds, monkeys, fish, and turtles.

How many ocelots are there?
Scientists think that there are about 1.5 to 3 million ocelots living in the wild.

Ocelots are wild cats that hunt other animals for food.

Ocelots in the Rain Forest

Ocelots are mammals. A mammal is a warm-blooded animal with a backbone. Warm-blooded animals have a body temperature that stays the same even when it is hot or cold outside. Temperature is a measure of heat or cold.

Ocelots are small wild cats. Their bodies are only about 3 feet (.9 m) long. Their name comes from an Aztec word that means field tiger. Aztecs are Mexican Indians. Other common names for the ocelot are tiger cat and leopard cat.

Ocelots are predators. Predators are animals that hunt and eat other animals. The animals that predators eat are called prey.

Ocelot Fur

Ocelots have colorful fur. It is yellow with dark brown stripes and spots. The brown spots are black around the edges. The shapes made by the spots and stripes are called **rosettes**. The rosettes run along the ocelot's body like chains.

Ocelots have dark bands of fur around their tails. The dark bands of fur look like rings. That is why they are called ringed tails.

Where Ocelots Live

Ocelots live in Central America, South America, and in southern parts of North America. Many live in and around the rain forests of South America. Rain forests are places where many trees and plants grow close together and much rain falls. Many different kinds of animals live in rain forests.

Ocelots can live in many different **habitats**. A habitat is a place where an animal or plant usually lives.

Many ocelots live in rain forests where trees and plants grow close together.

Many ocelots live in the Amazon rain forest. This is the largest rain forest in the world. It grows around the Amazon River in South America. Ocelots also live in grasslands, other forests, on mountains, and in marshes. Marshes are areas of wet, low land.

This ocelot is scratching a tree to mark its territory and sharpen its claws.

How Ocelots Live

Ocelots go into open places only at night. They usually stay in places thick with trees and grasses. Markings on an ocelot's fur act as **camouflage**. Camouflage is colors, shapes, and patterns that make something blend in with its background.

Ocelots make dens in thick grasses or fallen trees. A den is a small place like a cave where an animal lives. Some ocelots make dens in hollow tree trunks.

Both male and female ocelots have their own territories. A **territory** is land that an animal lives on and fights to keep for itself. Their territory can cover up to 3 square miles (7.8 square km). They mark their territories with their scents. Sometimes they also scratch trees to mark their territories. This warns other ocelots to stay away.

What Ocelots Look Like

Ocelots are small, wild cats. They have thin bodies and short tails. Females weigh 15 to 22 pounds (7 to 10 kg). Males weigh 20 to 35 pounds (9 to 15.9 kg). Large males can be 58 inches (150 cm) long from head to tail. Females are usually smaller than males.

Sometimes ocelots sleep high up in the branches of trees. Most wild cats are too big to hunt or sleep in small trees.

Like all cats, ocelots have sharp, retractable claws. Retractable means something can be pulled in or back. Ocelots can pull their claws back inside their paws. They can push them out when they want to hunt or climb trees.

Ocelots have large eyes. Large eyes help them see well in low light. Like other kinds of cats, ocelots see well at night.

Ocelots have strong jaws and legs. They use their jaws to catch and kill prey. They use their legs to climb, run, and swim. They are good swimmers.

Ocelots have large eyes that help them see well even when it is dark out.

This ocelot is hiding on a fallen tree to look for prey.

Hunting and Eating

Ocelots are carnivores. Carnivores are animals that eat only other animals. They hunt and eat mice, rats, birds, monkeys, fish, and turtles. They eat whatever they can catch. In different habitats, ocelots eat different kinds of prey.

Ocelots pluck birds before they eat them. Pluck means to pull the feathers out of a bird. They pluck birds using their paws and teeth.

Ocelots also eat **agoutis**. The agouti is a **rodent** the size of a big rat. Agoutis can weigh up to 9 pounds (4 kg).

Hunting

Ocelots are mostly nocturnal hunters. Nocturnal means they are active at night and sleep during the day. It is easier for ocelots to sneak up on prey at night. In the dark, they can see better than their prey.

An ocelot's body is good for climbing and hunting in trees. Their thin bodies allow them to fit into small spaces. They can climb trees to catch prey in only a few seconds.

Ocelots are very quiet when they hunt on the ground. They pull their claws inside their paws so they do not make noise. In the trees, they wait quietly on branches and listen for birds to land nearby.

Ocelots sleep during the day and hunt at night.

Ocelots form pairs during the mating season.

An Ocelot's Life Cycle

Ocelots usually live alone. They form pairs to mate. Both males and females can mate for many years. Females can mate when they are about 18 months old. They can have young until they are about 13 years old. Males can start mating when they are about 15 months old. They can mate until they are about 15 years old. Ocelots live from 13 to 15 years.

Mating takes place throughout the year in the rain forest. Females can mate every 4 to 6 months. They give off a special scent when they are ready to mate. Males follow the scent to the females.

This is a young ocelot kitten. It is learning how to sneak up on prey.

Cubs

Females look for hidden dens when they are ready to give birth. Dens help keep cubs safe from predators. Cubs are born about 70 days after mating. Females usually give birth to one or two cubs. Sometimes they have as many as three cubs.

Cubs look very much like their parents. Their yellow color is about the same. They also have spotted fur and ringed tails.

Mothers feed cubs for about two months. After two months, the mother takes the cubs hunting. She shows them how to catch and kill prey. At four months old, cubs are ready to hunt on their own.

Some people keep ocelots as pets.
Still, they should not taken from
their natural habitats.

Living with Ocelots

Ocelots can live near people. Some people even keep ocelots as pets. But they are not good pets. They give off a very strong smell. They will spray this smell on furniture and around houses. Because they are carnivores, they will kill chickens, dogs, and other small animals. They can also hurt small children.

Ocelots in Danger

People pay money for ocelot furs. They use the furs to make coats and other clothing. Every ocelot has different fur markings. This makes it hard for people to match furs for coats. That is why ocelot furs are expensive.

Ocelots that lose their rain forest homes might not have young again.

Hunting Ocelots

Hunting put ocelots in danger of dying out. It has been against the law to bring ocelot furs into the United States since 1972. It has been against the law to hunt ocelots in Peru and Colombia since 1973. Peru and Colombia are countries in South America.

Ocelots are still hunted in some countries where it is not against the law. In countries where it is against the law, some people still buy and sell ocelot furs. Hunting animals when it is against the law is called **poaching**. Poaching limits the number of animals in the wild.

Ocelots are also in danger of losing their habitat in the rain forest. Trees are being cut down to make room for homes and farms. Many kinds of animals lose their homes when this happens. Ocelots that lose their homes might not have young again.

Ocelots are in danger of dying out in their natural habitats.

Saving Ocelots

Ocelots are **endangered** animals. Endangered means in danger of dying out. In 1996, the United States Postal Service put pictures of endangered animals on U.S. stamps. The ocelot was one of them.

Ocelots need help from people to keep living in the wild. People must keep ocelot habitats safe. They must stop the buying and selling of ocelot furs. If people do not help ocelots, these animals may all die out.

Glossary

agouti (uh-GOO-tee)—a large rodent that lives in Central and South America and the West Indies

camouflage (KAM-uh-flahj)—colors, shapes, and patterns that make something blend in with its background

endangered (en-DAYN-jurd)—in danger of dying out

habitat (HAB-i-tat)—the place where an animal or plant usually lives

poaching (POH-ching)—to catch or kill fish or animals against the law

rodent (ROHD-uhnt)—a mammal with four special, sharp front teeth used for biting on things

rosette (roh-ZET)—a spot like a ring with smaller spots inside it

territory (TAYR-i-tor-ee)—land that an animal lives on and fights to keep for itself

Internet Sites

Big Cats.Com
http://www.bigcats.com

Big Cats Online
http://www.dialspace.dial.pipex.com/agarman
  /bco/ver4.htm

Discovery Channel
http://www.discovery.com

Useful Addresses

**Natural History Museum of Los Angeles
  County**
900 Exposition Boulevard
Los Angeles, CA 90007

Rainforest Action Network
2221 Pine Street, Suite 500
San Francisco, CA 94104

Index

agouti, 17
Amazon, 11
Aztec, 9

camouflage, 13
carnivore, 17, 25
Central America, 10
Colombia, 27

den, 13, 23

endangered, 29

habitat, 10, 17, 27, 29

leopard cat, 9

mammal, 9
marking, 13, 25
Mexican, 9

nocturnal, 18
North America, 10

Peru, 27
poach, 27
predator, 9, 23
prey, 9, 14, 17, 18, 23

retractable claws, 14
rodent, 17
rosette, 10

South America, 10, 11, 27

territory, 13
tiger cat, 9

United States, 27, 29

warm-blooded, 9